Contents

1 Only a Girl

Emmeline Pankhurst was born in 1858.
She was the daughter of a businessman,
and so the family was quite well off.
Her father was very fond of her,
but because she was a girl
he did not expect much for her.
He said 'What a pity she wasn't a boy'.

He did send her to school
with other girls from the same background.
When she was fifteen
she went to a school in Paris for two years.
She went to learn how to be a lady.

Her father did not expect that she would
need to work.
She would read, write, learn a little French,
how to sew and play the piano.
Like most girls she must prepare to be a wife.
A better education would be a waste.

Many people said that women could not cope
with politics and serious subjects.
Their brains were not up to it.
The school in Paris did teach her
a little more than that.
She learned some science and book keeping.

Emmeline Pankhurst aged 21.

2 Wife and Mother

When she was 18 she met Dr Pankhurst.
He was 20 years older than Emmeline,
but she loved him.
He treated her as an equal.
He said she had a good brain and should use it.

At that time, no women could vote
in general elections.

Dr Pankhurst said women should have
the right to vote.

Emmeline's father did not think that he was
the right man for her.
He didn't like the way
Emmeline was going to meetings
and even making speeches.

But Emmeline married Dr Pankhurst
and went on taking part in his work.

They had four children:
Christabel, Sylvia, Adela and Harry.

They treated their daughters and their son
in the same way.
They wanted the girls
to have the same chances as Harry.
All the children saw their mother
as a bright and active person
with work and interests outside the home.

Emmeline did voluntary work with the poor.
She also went to political meetings
with her husband.
They would take the children with them.
The Pankhursts were well known
in local politics.
In 1898 when Emmeline was 40 years old,
she took her daughter Christabel
to visit a friend in Switzerland.
After only a few days she had a message,
she was wanted back at home.

Emmeline left right away.
But on the train from London to Manchester,
she saw in a newspaper report
that her husband had died.
Now Emmeline had to look after
the family by herself.

She gave up her voluntary work
and took a paid office job.
She had to record all births
and deaths in the district.

She met many women and young girls
who had to bring up children
and had no money.
She met girls aged 13 who had babies.

She met one young mother
who was tried for murder.
She had let her baby die,
because she had no money to look after it.

Emmeline saw
that if women's lives were to get better,
they must have the vote.
If women won the right to vote
they could bring in laws
to make life better for all women.

Emmeline did not have much money.
But she wanted her children to do well.

Christabel went to study
for a degree in law.

At the time,
very few women went to University.
Even fewer studied law.
As a woman, she would not be able
to work as a lawyer.
It was thought to be a man's job.
But Emmeline said
she should do the degree anyway.

Sylvia went to art college.
All the girls wanted
to work for votes for women.

3 The Suffragettes

There were a few groups
trying to get votes for women.
But they were not getting anywhere.

They wrote letters, they signed petitions,
they had meetings and spoke to MPs.
But the Pankhurst women
wanted to try new tactics.

Christabel said they should start
a new group of their own.
It should be only for women.
It should be only for one thing:
'Votes for Women' – nothing else.
Emmeline agreed.
They had to shock people.
They had to make people listen.

Christabel and her friend
wanted to go to prison.
They got themselves arrested.

Emmeline Pankhurst being carried away by the police.

They were arrested
for spitting at a policeman.
They had to choose
to pay a fine or go to prison.
They chose prison.

They wanted to be in the news.
They spent five days in prison.
The newspapers reported it.

The Pankhursts started their own group.
They soon had many helpers.
Better off people gave money and
many gave their time to help.

People called them 'The Suffragettes'.
At first they tried
to get their message across
without breaking the law.

Emmeline led a march to Parliament
in pouring rain.

On this march, the Suffragettes wore
clothes of their own colours:
white, green and purple.
They also held a big rally in Hyde Park.
Five hundred thousand people turned up
to hear Emmeline speak.
But the government did not want to hear
about votes for women.
The Prime Minister was against it.

In Parliament the Suffragettes were mocked.
At meetings they were not allowed to speak.
Police tried to stop them
from going to Parliament.

At one of the marches,
there was a battle with the police.
Women were hit and pushed to the ground.
They got up and tried to go on.
They were hit again.
Some of them ended up in hospital.
Some ended up in prison.
The Suffragettes called this day
'Black Friday'.

Emmeline Pankhurst speaking in Hyde Park.

4 Prison

In prison, the Suffragettes did not give in.
Emmeline took the lead.
She would not go along with the petty rules.
She said she would not undress
in front of the warders.
She would not obey the rule of silence
in the exercise yard.
The prison warders
were not used to women like this.
They did not know what to do.

Some of the Suffragettes in prison
went on hunger strike.
They would not touch any food.
The hunger strikes were in the newspapers.
People felt sorry for the Suffragettes.

In prison, the warders tried
to make the women eat.
They force-fed them.
They pushed tubes down their throats.
The women were badly hurt.
They had bleeding mouths.
They choked, they got infections.

All this was bad for the government.
The women looked like helpless victims,
the government looked brutal.
Emmeline and her daughters were force-fed.
She wanted to show that she would not give in.
She believed in what she was fighting for.
She would do whatever was needed to win.

At the end of 1909, Emmeline went to America.
She made speeches to the public.
In America many people were fighting
for votes for women.
They were pleased to hear her speak.
But others said she was a hooligan.

In January 1910 Emmeline's son Harry died.
He was only 20,
but he had never been strong.
It was a great blow to lose him,
she was very sad.
But she did not give up her fight.
The work had to go on.

5 The Fight Goes On

Keeping to the law was not easy
when the law gave them no rights.
Christabel and Emmeline
wanted to step up the action.
They wanted to keep 'Votes for Women'
in the headlines.
They wanted to keep everyone talking about it.

Suffragettes broke the law more often.
They smashed windows in high street shops.
They smashed windows in public buildings.
They set fire to post boxes,
they vandalised golf courses with acid.

They damaged paintings in art galleries.
They cut telephone wires.
They sent letters full of pepper to MPs
who were against votes for women.
All over Britain, Suffragettes did the same.
Some of Emmeline's old friends
did not agree with these tactics.
Some of them had worked for votes for women
for a long time.

Emmeline and Christabel in prison uniform.

But they did not like these crimes.
There was a split in the group.
But Emmeline and her daughter, Christabel
stuck to their plan.
They said there was no other way.

Of course many women went to prison again.
They went on hunger strike again.
The government was worried.
What if one of these women died in prison?
It would be a great scandal.
The news would spread
all round the world.

So the government tried new tactics.
A new law said that if the women became ill
they should be let out of prison.
They could go home.

But when they were better,
they could be arrested again
to finish their sentence.
The Suffragettes called the new law
'The Cat and Mouse Act'.

In 1913 one of the Suffragettes was killed.
Her name was Emily Davison.

She went to the Derby Day horse race.
It was an important day.
The King's horse was in the race.
Emily jumped in front of the horse.
She wanted to stop the race.

She wanted the Suffragettes
to be in the news again.
The race was stopped.
But Emily Davison died from her injuries.

The Daily Mirror

THE MORNING JOURNAL WITH THE SECOND LARGEST NET SALE

No. 1,747.   Registered at the G. P. O. as a Newspaper.   THURSDAY, JUNE 3, 1909.   One Halfpenny.

"THESE VULGAR CREATURES FROM THE WEST END": MR. JOHN BURNS DENOUNCES THE SUFFRAGETTES AT WHITECHAPEL.

Mr. John Burns yesterday apologised to the East End of London for "these vulgar creatures from the West End." The President of the Local Government Board was opening an exhibition, arranged at the Whitechapel Art Gallery, under the auspices of the National Association for the Prevention of Consumption and Other Forms of Tuberculosis, and during his speech he was continually interrupted by suffragettes. It was these interruptions which called forth the apology. (1) Ejected suffragettes attempt to hold a meeting, but are prevented by the police. (2) A suffragette being ejected by two policemen. (3) Mr. Burns shouts "Put them out straightaway very quickly." (4) A suffragette leaving the Art Gallery after being ejected from the hall.—(*Daily Mirror* photographs.)

The *Daily Mirror* report on the Suffragettes.

In 1913 it was hard to tell
what would happen.
The government would not give in
and allow votes for women.
The Suffragettes would not give up their fight.
Emmeline was tired.
She had been in and out of prison.
She was getting older.
Her son had died,
her daughters did not agree about tactics.
Old friends said she was going too far.

The Suffragettes were split.
After all she had done
and all she had gone through,
women still did not have the vote.
But the Suffragettes
had kept up the pressure.
They had made people think about
votes for women.
Many people did not like the vandalism.
But many men and women
thought the Pankhursts had a case.

6 World War One

In 1914, Britain went to war in Europe.
Mrs Pankhurst had to make a choice.
Would she carry on fighting the government
in war time or would she support
the war effort?

Emmeline made up her mind.
In the testing time of war,
women must show
that they could be useful to the nation.

She called on the Suffragettes
to put aside their fight for the vote.
She told women everywhere
to show what they could do.
They must go into factories
and work for the war.
During the war,
women did all sorts of work
which men usually did.

Women police during World War One.

They drove trams and vans,
they carried coal, they made bombs.
There were women police
and women ambulance drivers.

At that time all of this was new.
Women did not do these things in peacetime.

The newspapers praised women's work.
Men could no longer say
a woman's place was just in the home.

But the war led to a split
in the Pankhurst family.
Sylvia did not agree with the war.
She said Britain should not be fighting.
She said people should not support
the war effort.

Emmeline was angry,
but Sylvia would not change her mind.
The two women never spoke again after this.

7 Victory

At the end of the war in 1918,
an Act of Parliament
gave women the right to vote.
Women had to be 30 to vote,
men could vote at 21.
But it was a start.

Women could also stand as MPs
for the first time.
It was ten years later when women
over 21 could vote.
Emmeline lived to see women over 21
win the vote.

But soon after that Act was passed in 1928
she became very ill.

Sylvia begged to go and see her.
Emmeline was dying, but she still refused.
She died in June 1928.
She was almost 70.

Some people say
that women won the right to vote
because of the war,
and not because of what the Suffragettes did.

But in other countries women had helped
in the same ways,
but they did not get the vote.

The long fight before the war
had helped to change people's minds.
Emmeline Pankhurst and her daughters
had made their case very strongly.

Many other brave women had fought
for the right to vote.
But it was Emmeline who was the leader.
She was someone they looked up to and followed.
She was very strong.

The right to vote was important
because women could go on
to make more changes.
They could change the laws to win equal pay,
better conditions for mothers and children,
equal chances in education and work,
more birth control.

Many of these changes
have made women's lives better.

Without the vote women had no power.
With the vote they had power.
That is what Emmeline Pankhurst believed
and that is why she would not give up,
until she had won.

Emmeline Pankhurst aged 69.